FOALS GROW UP TO BE HORSES

by Cecilia Minden, PhD

Cherry Lake Publishing • Ann Arbor, Michigan

1

Published in the United States of America
by Cherry Lake Publishing
Ann Arbor, Michigan
www.cherrylakepublishing.com

Photo Credits: Cover and page 1, ©Misza/Shutterstock, Inc.; page 4, ©Zuzule/Shutterstock, Inc.; page 6, ©Geoffrey Kuchera/Shutterstock, Inc.; page 8, ©Melissa Dockstader/Shutterstock, Inc.; page 10, ©Borgio/Dreamstime.com; page 12, ©iStockphoto.com/driftlessstudio; page 14, ©Lars Christensen/Shutterstock, Inc.; page 16, ©Lenkadan/Shutterstock, Inc.; page 18, ©Istockphoto.com/happyborder; page 20, ©Serna/Dreamstime.com

Library of Congress Cataloging-in-Publication Data
Minden, Cecilia.
Foals grow up to be horses/by Cecilia Minden.
p. cm.—(21st century basic skills library level 1)
Includes bibliographical references and index.
ISBN-13: 978-1-60279-853-3 (lib. bdg.)
ISBN-10: 1-60279-853-2 (lib. bdg.)
1. Foals—Juvenile literature. 2. Horses—Juvenile literature.
I. Title. II. Series.
SF302.M564 2010
636.1'07—dc22 2009048570

Cherry Lake Publishing would like to acknowledge the work of The Partnership for 21st Century Skills.
Please visit *www.21stcenturyskills.org* for more information.

Printed in the United States of America
Corporate Graphics Inc.
July 2010
CLFA07

TABLE OF CONTENTS

5 Foals
13 Growing Up
21 Horses

22 Find Out More
22 Glossary
23 Home and School Connection
24 Index
24 About the Author

Foals

Baby horses are called **foals**.

Many foals are born when
it is dark.

Foals have very long legs.

They can walk soon after they are born.

A foal gets milk from its mother.

Growing Up

Foals grow fast.

They need room to run.

Foals need clean water.

They like to eat grass and **oats**.

Foals also like **apples** and **carrots**.

Foals can see well.

They can even see in the dark!

Horses

Foals grow up to be horses.

It is fun to be with horses!

Find Out More

BOOK

Minden, Cecilia. *Farm Animals: Horses,* Ann Arbor, MI: Cherry Lake Publishing, 2010.

WEB SITE

Horses, Horse Pictures, Horse Facts—National Geographic
animals.nationalgeographic.com/animals/mammals/horse.html
Learn more about horses.

Glossary

apples (AP-uhlz) round, red fruits

carrots (KAR-ruhts) orange root vegetables

foals (FOLZ) young horses

oats (OHTS) grains of a kind of grass plant

Home and School Connection

Use this list of words from the book to help your child become a better reader. Word games and writing activities can help beginning readers reinforce literacy skills.

a
after
also
and
apples
are
baby
be
born
called
can
carrots
clean
dark
eat
even
fast
foal
foals
from
fun
gets
grass
grow
growing
have
horses
in
is
it
its
legs
like
long
many
milk
mother
need
oats
room
run
see
soon
the
they
to
up
very
walk
water
well
when
with

Index

apples, 17

birth, 7, 9

carrots, 17

darkness, 7, 19

food, 11, 15, 17

grass, 15
growing, 13, 21

horses, 5, 11, 21

legs, 9

milk, 11

oats, 15

running, 13

seeing, 19

walking, 9
water, 15

About the Author

Cecilia Minden is the former Director of the Language and Literacy Program at the Harvard Graduate School of Education. She currently works as a literacy consultant for school and library publishers and is the author of more than 100 books for children.